SECRETS TO PODCASTING

Secrets to Podcasting

KARL JOHNSON

Bald and Bonkers Network Academy

Contents

Introduction

Until recently, podcasting was a concept unfamiliar to many. Now, it's a topic of daily conversation, with people avidly discussing and sharing their favorite shows on social media.

For those who haven't been sequestered away from the digital world, podcasts are likely a familiar form of entertainment and education. They serve as excellent companions, whether you're engaged in other activities or simply relaxing.

The true allure of podcasting lies in its versatility. You could be commuting, exercising, or performing any number of tasks, all while absorbing new information from your preferred podcast hosts. The medium liberates you from the confines of a desk or the small screen of a mobile device.

Podcasting offers unparalleled freedom, allowing you to choose your content, listen at your convenience, and tailor the experience to your preferences. These are just a few of the many advantages of this modern medium.

For entrepreneurs and content creators, podcasting holds significant meaning. It represents an opportunity to engage with audiences on a deeper level. The decision to start a podcast should not be taken lightly, given its potential impact.

This comprehensive guide is designed to unveil the intricacies of podcast creation. Prepare to jot down key points as we delve into the journey of crafting a successful and lucrative podcast series.

Chapter 1

Choosing a Niche

To maximize your chances of success, it's crucial to find the perfect niche for your podcast. This step, while it may seem counterintuitive at first, is essential.

You might wonder, "Why limit my audience by niching down when I can reach anyone across the globe with my podcast?"

Consider this: there are hundreds of thousands of podcasts out there. How will you differentiate yours? Certainly not by being a jack-of-all-trades podcaster.

Creating a podcast that covers every topic imaginable is unlikely to lead to success. People trust experts.

Podcasts that focus on a specific niche tend to attract more followers than those that do not. Specializing in a particular area allows you to establish yourself or your brand as an authoritative figure.

For example, if your goal is to be recognized as an expert in email marketing, launching a podcast dedicated to this subject would be beneficial. Similarly, if your expertise lies in social media marketing, starting a podcast focused on that niche would be advantageous. If you are passionate about digital marketing, creating a podcast that explores various aspects of this field could be a way to share your knowledge.

By choosing a niche you are knowledgeable about, you can effectively position yourself as a specialist, offering valuable insights and strategies to your audience. People love to listen to authority figures. When you select a niche, you need to stick to that niche, creating content that fits within it. Over time, people will come to recognize that you are true to your word and truly an expert in your niche.

You can't ever prove you're an expert if you jump from one niche to another. You will end up confusing your listeners. For instance, they may have followed you because you gave out a lot of good advice in your social media episodes. However, if over the next ten episodes you talk about auto-detailing, crocheting, or fishing, you'll likely have people unfollowing you and leaving bad reviews on your podcast. This will damage your reputation and your brand. If you want to be recognized as an expert and a trustworthy authority, you need to pick the right niche.

Picking the Right Niche

Niche selection can either be straightforward or difficult. It all depends on your needs and preferences. If you want to take the easy route, just pick a niche you love, something you know you can create tons of content about, and stick to that.

However, if you have a lot of different interests, here's a technique you can use to figure out the right niche for your podcast.

Step 1: Write Down Your Interests and Passions

What are you passionate about? What topics interest you the most? What industry are you most knowledgeable about?

Come up with a list of 5-10 potential niches. This step is extremely important because if you choose the wrong niche, you will eventually lose interest in continuing your podcast. You'd run out of ideas to keep your show going. Your disinterest and lack of passion will be evident in your show. People are astute listeners and can tell when someone is passionate about a topic or not. So, if you want your podcast to succeed, you need to get this step right.

Step 2: Identify the Problems You Can Solve

Write down the problems you can solve in each of the potential niches you've identified in Step 1. You can come up with possible problems off the top of your head, which should be easy if you know the topic. But if you need more ideas, there are tons of resources you can check online.

You can go on Quora or Yahoo Answers and check out what kind of questions people are asking in your potential niches. Visit forums and social media groups as well. These places provide lots of free information for anyone willing to look. You can even use Google Suggest and other keyword tools to determine if people are searching for solutions to specific problems.

Step 3: Analyze Your Competition

Whatever niche you decide on, you will most likely have some competition. There's no need to be afraid of going after 'saturated' or high-competition niches. Figure out what everyone else is doing and see if you can come up with your own angle. That 'angle' will be your edge, helping you stand out from the crowd.

Check your competitors' podcasts. How many followers do they have? What topics are they covering? Do you think you can one-up them and do a better job?

Step 4: Choose the Right Niche

Some people may say Step 4 should be devoted to checking if a niche is profitable. However, with podcasting, there are many different ways you can monetize your podcast. We'll cover monetization later, but for now, you should know that selecting your niche and growing your audience are the most important things you should focus on first. Monetization is something you shouldn't worry about when you're just starting a podcast.

With that said, the information you collected in Steps 1-3 should now give you an idea of your perfect niche. Your gut will probably tell you which niche is right for you.

The important thing is that you must enjoy talking about your topic. Otherwise, you risk losing your motivation to continue with your podcast a few weeks or months from now.

Conclusion

To sum up, take the time to figure out the right niche for your podcast. Doing so will increase your chances of success in the long run.

Chapter 2

Branding

Branding is much more than just choosing a catchy name for your podcast or designing the perfect cover art. It is essentially how you want people to recognize and remember your podcast. If you build your brand correctly, you'll reap the benefits for a long time to come.

Define Your Podcast's Mission and Vision

When starting out, it's important to identify your podcast's mission and vision. These elements guide the type of content you create and help shape your brand.

Mission Statement: This outlines your podcast's goals and how you intend to achieve them. It's all about what your podcast aims to do in the present.

Vision Statement: This is what you want your podcast to become in the future. It's your long-term aspiration.

Ensuring that every episode aligns with your mission and vision is crucial. This consistency helps build your brand and defines what you want to be known for.

Establish Your Podcast's Voice and Personality

Your uniqueness is your strength. You don't want to sound like anyone else but yourself. This is how you create your own special brand.

Start by being as natural as possible. When recording your episodes, speak as you would in real life. Authenticity resonates with listeners. Depending on your audience, you may want to adjust your language, but your natural style should always shine through. For example, if you want your show to be known for its colorful language, go for it, but make sure it fits your brand.

Creating a catchy tagline can also help. Think of a tagline that represents your show well, and be unique and creative. Bring your voice and personality to each episode.

Consistency Matters

Your branding shouldn't be limited to your podcast alone. It should be consistent across all platforms you use, whether it's your blog, YouTube channel, or Facebook fan page.

Use your podcast cover art as a banner on your website or as your profile picture on social media. The goal is to avoid any disconnect when people find you on different platforms. You want people to recognize your brand wherever they go. For instance, if you're promoting your podcast on your blog, make sure your branding is consistent across Apple Podcast, Spotify, and TuneIn. This way, when people visit these platforms, they will recognize your brand immediately. Consistency in branding activities encourages people to follow you on multiple platforms.

Build a Community Around Your Brand

People love feeling like they belong to a community. Take John Lee Dumas' podcast "Entrepreneurs On Fire" as an example; he addresses his listeners as "Fire Nation." That's branding in action.

Once you've built a following, you can create a sense of community by giving your listeners a collective identity. If you already have an established brand elsewhere, use the same name for your podcast listeners. If not, setting up profiles on other platforms can help unify your branding efforts.

Building a community allows your listeners to feel like they belong. It helps create a relationship with your audience, making them feel special. To achieve this, you need to understand your listeners well. By knowing who they are, you can provide the right solutions to the right people, enhancing their sense of belonging and loyalty to your brand.

In summary, effective branding involves defining your mission and vision, establishing a unique voice and personality, maintaining consistency across platforms, and building a community. By following these steps, you can create a strong brand that will attract and retain a loyal audience.

Chapter 3

Equipment

Essential Podcasting Equipment: What You Need to Know

Embarking on your podcasting journey requires more than just a passion for sharing your voice; it requires the right equipment. While it's possible to start a podcast with minimal investment, a small financial outlay is necessary to ensure your podcast sounds professional and engaging.

Investing in Quality Podcasting Equipment

It's a common misconception that you can start a podcast without spending any money. While you don't need to invest a fortune, you will need to allocate some budget to get the ball rolling. Many successful podcasters have managed to launch their shows with equipment costing less than $100. Here are the essential tools you need:

1.   **Microphone** A high-quality microphone is crucial for achieving professional-sounding audio. While built-in microphones on laptops or phones can be used in a pinch, they won't provide the clarity and depth needed for a professional podcast. Consider investing in an affordable yet high-quality USB microphone.

2.   **Pop Filter** A pop filter is a simple and inexpensive tool that can significantly improve your audio quality by filtering out plosive sounds from consonants like "d," "p," "g," and "b." This helps prevent

annoying popping sounds that can distract listeners. Pop filters are available for under $10 on Amazon.

3. **Audio Software** You'll need software to record and edit your podcast. Fortunately, there are excellent free options available for all operating systems:

    - **Audacity:** This open-source software is full-featured and cross-platform. It may look intimidating initially, but it offers robust functionality for recording and editing your podcast. You can add intros, outros, and various effects to your recordings. Here is the link to find Audacity: https://www.audacityteam.org/download/windows/
    - **GarageBand:** Pre-installed on Mac computers, GarageBand is user-friendly and intuitive, making it easy to create professional-sounding podcasts without additional cost.

4. **Graphics Software** Eye-catching cover

art is essential for attracting listeners. If you're not skilled in graphic design, consider using tools like Canva to create your podcast cover art. For inspiration, look at other podcasts in your niche and find ways to make your cover stand out. Alternatively, you might hire a designer if your budget allows.

5.   **Headphones** Good headphones are vital for monitoring your recordings and editing your podcast. They help you hear how you sound during recording, allowing you to adjust your voice, volume, and speed in real-time. Over-the-ear headphones are generally preferred for their comfort and hygiene, especially if you have guests in your studio. Quality headphones also make editing easier, enabling you to catch and remove unwanted sounds more efficiently.

Conclusion

Investing in the right podcasting equipment is essential for producing a professional and engaging podcast. By allocating a modest budget to these essential tools, you can significantly enhance the quality of your podcast and create a more enjoyable experience for your listeners. Whether you're starting with a minimal setup or gradually upgrading your equipment, the key is to focus on the essentials that will help you deliver high-quality audio and compelling content.

Chapter 4

Planning

ENSURING YOUR PODCAST'S LONGEVITY: THE IMPORTANCE OF ADVANCED PLANNING

To ensure your podcast remains engaging and doesn't lose momentum, it is crucial to plan your episodes well in advance. Ideally, you should outline your content for weeks or even months ahead. If you're particularly ambitious, planning for a full year can be highly beneficial.

The Importance of Advanced Planning

Advanced planning brings numerous advantages. If you underestimate the effort required to consistently generate fresh podcast topics, you may quickly find yourself struggling for content. Without proper planning, you risk repeating ideas, which can cause your audience to lose interest and unfollow your podcast. This can be avoided by having a well-thought-out content strategy.

By planning ahead, you gain a comprehensive view of your podcast's content trajectory. This allows you to ensure that each episode aligns with your overall mission and vision. If you notice deviations, you can adjust your upcoming episodes accordingly to stay on track. Additionally, advanced planning helps you balance your content, ensuring a mix of themes and topics that cater to your audience's diverse interests.

Commitment is Key

Regardless of how meticulously you plan your content, without the discipline and commitment to follow through, your efforts may go to waste. One common pitfall for many podcasters is the lack of sustained commitment, especially when faced with challenges.

Commitment is essential for maintaining a consistent podcasting schedule. Determine what you aim to achieve with your podcast—whether it's brand promotion, generating additional income, or attracting qualified leads for your business. Having a clear goal will help maintain your focus and drive. Remember, podcasting involves significant effort and planning, and the right mindset is essential for long-term success.

Organizing Your Content

There are several effective methods to organize your podcast content. Whether you prefer traditional pen and paper or modern digital tools, the key is to find a system that works for you. Here are some strategies:

Content or Editorial Calendar

A content or editorial calendar is invaluable for content creators, including podcasters. It helps you organize your content and stream-line your workflow. One highly recommended tool for this purpose is Google Calendar. With a Google account, you can create multiple calendars, assign different colors to each, and manage them effortlessly. This allows you to keep track of various aspects of your content strategy, from podcast episodes to social media posts.

Google Calendar also enables you to add detailed descriptions, notes, and attachments to each calendar entry. This feature is particularly useful for planning podcast episodes, ensuring you have all necessary information and materials organized in one place. By using a content calendar, you can plan episodes in advance and keep your audience engaged with consistent, high-quality content.

Brainstorming Episode Topics

Effective brainstorming is essential for generating fresh and engaging podcast topics. Set aside dedicated time for brainstorming, either alone or with your team. There are several techniques you can use:

- **Group Brainstorming**: Gather your team or co-hosts and encourage everyone to share ideas. You can do this verbally or by having each person write down their thoughts within a set time frame. Incentives can motivate the group to generate innovative ideas.
- **Solo Brainstorming**: Use techniques like associative brainstorming, where you write down everything you associate with a specific topic. Alternatively, try word storming, where you list all the words that come to mind when you see another word. Visual thinkers may find mind mapping helpful to show relationships between ideas and develop themes for multiple episodes.

Research your topics thoroughly, ask questions in online forums, and engage with your audience to gather insights and ideas.

Outlining or Scripting Episodes

Whether you prefer outlines or scripts, having a structured approach to each episode is crucial. A detailed outline or script helps you maintain a smooth flow from one point to another, minimizing pauses and reducing the need for extensive editing.

Experiment with both methods to determine which works best for you. Start with an outline for one episode, then try a script for another. Evaluate the time taken from writing to the finished, edited audio. This will help you identify the most efficient approach for producing high-quality content.

Conclusion

By organizing your content in advance and experimenting with different processes, you can develop a system that works for you. This will enable you to consistently produce engaging and professional podcast episodes, ensuring the long-term success of your show. Advanced planning, commitment, and effective content organization are the cornerstones of a successful podcasting strategy.

Chapter 5

Recording and Editing
Like a Pro

Ensuring High-Quality Podcast Audio Recording and Editing

Your podcast will be judged by the quality of your audio recording and your content. Assuming you have thoroughly researched your topic, the next crucial step is to record and edit your podcast audio professionally. A well-produced podcast makes a positive impression on your listeners, while subpar and poorly edited audio can drive them away.

Recording Done Correctly

To avoid extensive editing sessions, it is essential to record your audio correctly from the start. Fixing recording mistakes is a common nightmare for podcasters, and sometimes it might even be easier to record the entire episode from scratch. While achieving an error-free recording may not be possible in your initial episodes, you can certainly minimize your editing time by following these techniques:

Record in a Quiet Place

Find a quiet place to record your episode. Close all doors and windows, and put your phone on silent mode. You don't need a lot of tools to record a show. Simply plug in your microphone (with a pop filter) to your laptop, put on a pair of headphones or earphones, hit Record, and start talking. However, if you record in a noisy environment, you'll face a tough time editing out all that background noise later on.

Speak Clearly into Your Microphone

Using a good headset will help you monitor how you sound. Without it, you won't know if you're speaking too softly, too loudly, or if your breathing is distracting. If you can't hear yourself clearly through your headphones, you may need to adjust your recording software's settings. A headset allows you to tweak your tone, cadence, and volume as you speak into your microphone.

Don't Share Microphones

If you have a co-host or a guest, ensure each person uses a separate microphone. Sharing a microphone can complicate the editing process, making it difficult to balance the volume of different voices. Although placing a microphone in the middle might seem like a solution, it often results in uneven audio levels, leading to more editing work.

Do a Test Recording

Before recording a full episode, conduct a

test recording. It's easy to overlook basic steps in your nervousness, such as plugging in the microphone or unmuting it. Check everything —microphones, room acoustics, recording software, headphones—to avoid errors that could disrupt your recording.

Editing Audio Like a Pro

Your listeners should have a pleasant experience while listening to your podcast. Background noises, heavy breathing, or other distractions can drive listeners away and result in negative reviews. To avoid this, listen to the entire audio file, not just the waveform on your screen. The editing process varies between software, so familiarize yourself with your chosen software through manuals or YouTube tutorials.

Stitching Your Final Audio File

Once you are satisfied with your edited recording, the next step is to stitch your intro, outro, and main episode audio into a single file. This final audio file is what you will upload to your podcast hosting service. Ensure everything sounds good before hitting the Upload button.

Adding Metadata or ID3 Tags

Before uploading your audio file, add metadata or ID3 tags. These details provide listeners with important information about your show, such as episode number, episode title, podcast name, and summary. Free programs like Easy-Tag: https://wiki.gnome.org/Apps/EasyTAG and MP3Tag: https://www.mp3tag.de/en can help you add metadata to your podcast file.

By following these guidelines, you can ensure your podcast is professionally recorded and edited, enhancing the listening experience for your audience and increasing the chances of retaining and growing your listener base.

Chapter 6

Finding a Host

Hosting Your Podcast Audio Files

For your podcast to reach listeners, it needs to be hosted on a suitable platform where it can be streamed or downloaded. Audio files, especially those of high quality and lengthy episodes, can be quite large, so selecting the right host is essential to accommodate your podcasting needs.

Using a Web Hosting Service

Many web hosting services advertise "unlimited" storage space. However, this is typically intended for website files only. Podcast audio files are media files, and uploading them to your web hosting server (especially on a shared hosting plan) can result in severe penalties or even service termination.

The exception to this rule is if you are on an expensive, dedicated web hosting plan, which essentially means renting an entire server from your web host. In such cases, you may be able to upload your podcast files to your web server. However, each hosting company has its own Terms and Conditions, so it's best to confirm with them first to avoid potential issues.

Another downside to using a web hosting service is that when your server goes down, both your website and podcast will be inaccessible. Listeners on platforms like Apple Podcasts or Spotify will be cut off, leading to frustration and potentially losing your audience. Therefore, it's wise to host your website and podcast files separately to prevent one service's downtime from affecting the other.

Using a Podcast or Media Hosting Service

Podcast or media hosting services exist for a reason. They are not direct competitors to web hosting companies because they offer specialized services optimized for hosting and serving large media files. Here are some benefits of using a media hosting service for your podcast:

Podcast RSS Feed

Podcast hosting services are designed specifically for hosting audio files and are optimized for podcasts. They provide built-in, validated RSS feeds that comply with all major podcast directories, simplifying the submission process. Simply grab your RSS feed link and paste it into the podcast submission forms on platforms like Apple Podcasts, Google Podcasts, Spotify, Stitcher, TuneIn, PodBean, and SoundCloud.

When you upload a new episode to your hosting account, all directories where you've submitted your RSS feed will automatically receive the update. Your followers will also receive your new episodes on their preferred devices without any extra effort from you.

Podcast Statistics

One significant advantage of using a media/podcast hosting service is access to detailed statistics about your show, which is typically not available from web hosting companies. Depending on the service provider, you can gain insights such as total and unique downloads, the apps listeners use to tune into your show, traffic sources, the geographical location of your listeners, and more.

This detailed information is invaluable, especially if you're seeking sponsorships. Brands and businesses often ask for audience demographics, and with a dedicated podcast hosting service, you can provide accurate data with just a few clicks.

Podcast Page

If you don't have an existing blog or website, many podcast hosting companies offer a free podcast page. This page serves as a hub for your podcast, where you can add banners, show notes, social media channels, and more. If you already have a blog, you can link your podcast page to your blog, which can benefit your blog's SEO.

The podcast page typically includes a free media player, allowing visitors to stream your show directly from their browsers. They can also download, subscribe, and share your podcast easily.

Affordable Plans

Pricing is an important factor when choosing a suitable host for your podcast. Some hosts offer free plans for those new to podcasting. For example, BuzzSprout: https://www.buzzsprout.com/ allows you to upload up to 2 hours of audio each month for free. However, free plans can limit your podcast's growth, as they may host episodes for only a short period. Services like Spotify for Podcasters: https://podcasters.spotify.com/, Acast: https://www.acast.com/, and Redbubble: https://www.redbubble.com/ also offer free plans but may charge for advanced features.

For serious podcasters, subscribing to a paid service is recommended. Basic plans can be as low as $3 on PodBean: https://www.podbean.com/ and $5 on Libsyn: https://www.libsyn.com/. If you need more storage or bandwidth, you can easily upgrade to a higher pricing tier without any downtime.

Conclusion

Choosing the right hosting service for your podcast can save you from numerous headaches and help propel your podcast to success. By selecting a dedicated podcast hosting service, you can ensure your audio files are managed efficiently, your listeners are happy, and you have access to valuable insights about your audience.

Chapter 7

Launch!

Launching Your Podcast Like a Rocket Ship

Congratulations on recording and uploading your podcast episodes! Now, it's time to spread the word and launch your podcast like a pro. Here are some effective strategies to get started:

Submit to Podcast Directories

Submitting your podcast to various directories is crucial to reaching a wider audience. While iTunes and Google Podcasts are popular, don't limit yourself. Submit your show to platforms like Spotify, Stitcher, TuneIn, SoundCloud, and more. This initial effort only takes a few hours but can yield immense returns in terms of listenership later on.

Utilize Your Personal Network

Start promoting your podcast within your personal network of family, friends, colleagues, and acquaintances. Share your excitement about the value your podcast offers and ask them to support you by listening and leaving reviews. Positive reviews on platforms like iTunes can significantly boost your podcast's visibility and credibility in a review-driven world.

Leverage Your Blog or Podcast Page

If you have an existing blog, leverage it to promote your podcast. Send out email notifications to subscribers, write blog posts introducing your new podcast episodes, and embed media players to facilitate easy listening and downloading. Having your own blog or podcast page not only enhances visibility but also provides flexibility in content presentation, including show notes, transcripts, and embedded videos.

Collaborate with Influencers

Influencer marketing can amplify your podcast's reach. Identify influencers in your niche who have a genuine and engaged following. Avoid influencers with low engagement rates, which may indicate fake followers. Collaborate with influencers to promote your podcast through their social media channels, blogs, or podcasts, reaching their loyal audience and potentially gaining new listeners.

Interview Industry Experts

Invite experts relevant to your podcast's theme for interviews. Aim for experts with established followings as their endorsement can attract their audience to your show. Provide them with promotional materials like customized swipe files for easy sharing on social media and other platforms. Express gratitude and openness to reciprocate by participating in their content, further expanding your reach and credibility.

Paid Advertising

Consider investing in targeted ads on platforms like Facebook Ads to reach your ideal audience effectively. Understand your audience demographics to optimize ad targeting and maximize engagement. If unfamiliar with ad management, explore other platforms or seek assistance to ensure cost-effective promotion of your podcast.

Conclusion

Launching your podcast requires strategic promotion across multiple channels. By leveraging podcast directories, personal networks, blogs, influencer collaborations, expert interviews, and targeted ads, you can effectively increase your podcast's visibility and attract a loyal audience. Consistent promotion and engagement will ultimately propel your podcast to success.

Chapter 8

Plug Products and Services

Maximizing Product and Service Promotion on Your Podcast

Promoting your products and services on your podcast is not only acceptable but a smart business move. However, to achieve a good conversion rate without turning off your audience, here are some effective strategies to consider:

Be Subtle and Strategic

When you're starting out with your podcast, avoid being overly sales-oriented. Instead, focus on building trust and providing value to your listeners. Integrate mentions of your products or services naturally into your podcast episodes. For example, in your podcast introduction, briefly mention your credentials and the availability of your courses or books on platforms like Amazon or Udemy. Encourage listeners to explore the show notes for more information, maintaining a non-intrusive approach.

Similarly, when concluding your show, subtly remind your audience about your offerings and provide a link for further details. By adopting a respectful and informative tone, you intrigue listeners without overwhelming them with sales pitches.

Always Provide Value

Avoid the stereotype of aggressive sales tactics by consistently prioritizing your audience's needs and interests. Address their pain points during your podcast episodes and demonstrate how your products or services can provide effective solutions. Instead of simply urging listeners to purchase, explain the specific benefits they can expect and offer practical guidance on using your offerings to achieve desired outcomes.

By focusing on educating and empowering your audience, you establish credibility and foster genuine interest in your offerings. This approach not only enhances engagement but also builds a foundation for long-term customer relationships.

Offer Alternatives and Promote Others

In instances where your products or services may not directly align with a particular podcast episode's theme, consider promoting alternative solutions. This could include affiliate products or even products from competitors that meet your audience's needs effectively. This demonstrates a commitment to providing valuable recommendations, irrespective of direct financial gain.

Additionally, reach out to competitors or complementary businesses and inform them about your podcast. Building positive relationships within your industry can lead to reciprocal promotion opportunities and further expand your audience reach.

Conclusion

Effectively promoting your products and services on your podcast involves maintaining a balance between subtle promotion and delivering genuine value to your audience. By focusing on their needs, offering insightful solutions, and occasionally promoting alternatives, you can enhance listener engagement, increase conversions, and establish your podcast as a trusted resource within your niche. This strategic approach not only benefits your business but also enriches the overall podcasting experience for your audience.

Chapter 9

Growing Your Audience

Strategies for Growing Your Podcast Audience

Growing your podcast audience requires dedication and strategic planning. Here are some proven techniques to effectively expand your listener base:

Consistency is Key

Similar to nurturing a chia pet, achieving podcast success demands consistency. Whether you release episodes weekly, bi-weekly, or daily, sticking to a reliable schedule is crucial. Consistency builds anticipation among your audience, making your podcast a regular part of their routines. For example, if you commit to publishing every Monday, your listeners will anticipate new episodes during their commute or daily walks with their pets.

To maintain consistency, consider recording episodes in advance. This allows flexibility for holidays or emergencies, ensuring uninterrupted content delivery and a loyal following.

Reviews and Ratings Matter

Positive reviews and ratings significantly impact a podcast's visibility and credibility. Encourage listeners to leave reviews on platforms like iTunes or wherever your podcast is hosted. Positive reviews attract new listeners, while negative feedback can provide valuable insights for improvement.

If you receive negative reviews, handle them professionally. Respond respectfully to valid criticism and consider flagging inappropriate reviews. Use constructive feedback to enhance future episodes, ensuring continuous improvement in content quality.

Hold Engaging Contests

Engage your audience by hosting contests related to your podcast. Contests can encourage listeners to leave reviews, share on social media, or suggest taglines for your show. Offer enticing prizes such as access to online courses or branded merchandise. Multiple winners or personalized rewards like interviews or promotional spots can further boost engagement and loyalty.

Strategic Promotion

Allocate time to promote your podcast effectively. Experts suggest dedicating 20-30% of your effort to content creation and the remainder to promotion. Identify your target audience and their preferred platforms. Utilize tools like the Facebook Pixel to retarget visitors to your website with tailored Facebook Ads, increasing engagement among warm leads already familiar with your brand.

Understanding where your audience spends time online allows you to strategically place your content and ads, maximizing visibility and engagement. Whether targeting younger demographics on social media or older audiences through forums and newsletters, effective promotion is key to expanding your podcast's reach.

Conclusion

By maintaining consistency, actively seeking reviews, hosting engaging contests, and strategically promoting your content, you can effectively grow your podcast audience. These strategies not only attract new listeners but also foster long-term engagement and loyalty. Implementing these tactics will help you establish a strong presence in the competitive podcasting landscape and achieve sustainable growth over time.

Chapter 10

Landings Sponsors
and Advertisers

Strategies for Attracting Advertisers
and Sponsors to Your Podcast

Building a successful podcast involves more than just creating content; it requires cultivating a loyal audience and attracting appropriate advertisers and sponsors. Here's how you can strategically approach sponsorship opportunities:

Focus on Community, Not Money

The foundation of a successful podcast lies

in nurturing a community of dedicated listeners who value your content. Avoid making money your primary motivation. Instead, focus on delivering valuable insights and solutions that resonate with your target audience. Building a loyal community ensures sustainable growth and attracts sponsors interested in engaging with your dedicated listenership.

Steps to Attract Advertisers and Sponsors

1. Build a Solid Following

Aim to grow your podcast audience to a substantial size, typically between 5,000 to 10,000 listeners, before actively seeking sponsors. A larger following increases your appeal to potential sponsors, who may even approach you once your podcast gains popularity. Focus on consistent content delivery and engagement strategies to organically grow your listener base.

2. Foster Listener Engagement

Advertisers and sponsors value engaged

audiences. Monitor listener feedback through reviews on platforms like iTunes and social media interactions. Positive engagement metrics demonstrate audience interest and influence sponsor decisions. Maintain active social media channels and encourage audience interaction to showcase your podcast's community engagement.

3. Uphold Integrity

Maintain a reputation for integrity and authenticity. Sponsors prefer podcasters who align with their brand values and demonstrate trustworthiness. Avoid compromising your integrity for financial gain; prioritize sponsorships that genuinely benefit your audience. Transparency in sponsor selection and willingness to decline mismatched sponsors uphold your podcast's credibility and long-term success.

4. Provide Excellent Customer Service

Sponsorship involves a level of customer service. Ensure sponsors feel valued and appreciated by delivering on promises and exceeding expectations. Underpromise and over-deliver to build trust and satisfaction. Positive sponsor experiences foster lasting relationships and may lead to future sponsorship opportunities or referrals.

Conclusion

By prioritizing community building over monetary gain, attracting the right advertisers and sponsors becomes a natural progression for your podcast. Focus on growing your audience, fostering engagement, upholding integrity, and delivering exceptional customer service. These strategies not only enhance sponsor satisfaction but also maintain the trust and loyalty of your listeners, ensuring sustainable growth and success for your podcast endeavors.

Conclusion

Earning revenue from your podcast is achievable, yet it requires patience and dedication. Podcasting is not a quick path to wealth; success in this field demands a thorough understanding of the medium. Commitment to producing content that resonates with your intended audience is key. By cultivating and engaging with your listeners, you can eventually realize substantial profits through podcasting.

Checklist for Establishing Your Podcast

Choosing Your Podcast Niche

Why Niche Down?

- Authority and Trust: Establish your-self as an expert.
- Audience Engagement: Solve specific problems.

Steps to Pick the Right Niche:

1. Identify Interests: List 5-10 potential niches.
2. Problem Solving: Research issues on Q&A sites, forums, and social media.
3. Analyze Competition: Understand competitors' strategies and find your unique angle.
4. Choose Wisely: Decide based on inter-

ests, problem-solving potential, and competition analysis.

Podcast Branding

Mission and Goals:

- Define your podcast's purpose and objectives.
- Plan strategies to achieve these goals effectively.

Vision and Voice:

- Envision the future of your podcast.
- Maintain authenticity and a consistent personality.
- Craft a catchy tagline that reflects your uniqueness.

Consistency Across Platforms:

- Ensure uniform branding on social media, blogs, and podcast directories.

- Build a community where your audience feels a sense of belonging.

Podcasting Equipment

Microphone Quality:

- Invest in a quality microphones and headsets.
- Bald and Bonkers Network LLC hosts an Amazon Shop earning commissions from sales that offers an extensive list of podcasting equipment recommendations: https://amzn.to/4f6igTl

Additional Equipment:

- Use a pop filter to reduce plosive sounds.
- Consider headphones for monitoring and editing.

Planning and Organizing Content

Effective Planning:

- Maintain a content calendar for podcasts, social media, and blog posts.
- Brainstorm episode topics using techniques like mind mapping and associative brainstorming.
- Develop outlines or scripts to structure each episode effectively.

Recording and Editing

Recording Tips:

- Record in a quiet environment with clear speech.
- Avoid sharing microphones and conduct test recordings.

Editing Techniques:

- Edit efficiently by focusing on removing noise and normalizing volume.
- Add intros, outros, and metadata tags to enhance professionalism.

Podcast Hosting and Launch

Choosing a Host:

- Opt for a podcast hosting service for optimized performance and easy RSS feed management.

Launching Your Podcast:

- Submit to major directories like Apple Podcasts, Google Play, and Spotify.
- Leverage personal networks, blogs, and social media for initial promotion.

Growing Your Audience

Audience Engagement:

- Encourage reviews and ratings to build credibility.
- Hold contests and giveaways to increase listener interaction.

Promotion Strategies:

- Allocate 80% of your efforts to pro-

moting content via social media, email, and ads.
- Utilize Facebook Pixel for targeted marketing to warm leads.

Attracting Advertisers and Sponsors

Criteria for Sponsorship:

- Maintain a solid listener base of 5,000 to 10,000.
- Focus on listener engagement and positive feedback.
- Uphold integrity by aligning with sponsors that resonate with your audience.

Customer Service Approach:

- Underpromise and overdeliver to exceed sponsor expectations.
- Integrate subtle product mentions in intros or outros, prioritizing audience value.

By following these steps and strategies, you can establish, grow, and sustain a

successful podcast that resonates with your audience and attracts meaningful partner-
ships.